Pastors, Politics & Paranoia

Putting an End to the Crisis of Silence

by Pastor Joel L. Rissinger

Copyright © 2026 by Joel L. Rissinger

All rights reserved. No part of this book may be reproduced or transmitted in any form or by any means, electronic or mechanical, including: photocopying, recording, or by any information storage and retrieval system, without permission in writing from the copyright owner. This work is based on the experiences of an individual. Every effort has been made to ensure the accuracy of the content.

Pastors, Politics & Paranoia
Putting an End to the Crisis of Silence

Author: Joel L. Rissinger
Editor: Lyda Rose Haerle
Cover and Interior Layout: Griffin Mill

Unless otherwise indicated, Scripture quotations are taken from the HOLY BIBLE, NEW KING JAMES VERSION®. Copyright © 1982 by Thomas Nelson. Used by permission. All rights reserved.

ISBN: 978-1-957351-89-6

PUBLISHED BY NICO 11 PUBLISHING & DESIGN,
MUKWONAGO, WISCONSIN
MICHAEL NICLOY, PUBLISHER
www.nico11publishing.com

Quantity and wholesale order requests can be emailed to:
mike@nico11publishing.com

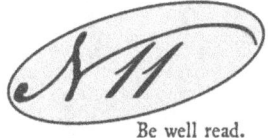

Be well read.

Printed in The United States of America

Pastors, Politics & Paranoia

Table of Contents

Foreword by Dr. Kevin McGary..................9
Introduction..................13
Part One: The Foundation of Fear..................17
Chapter One: What ARE We Afraid Of?..................19
Chapter Two: Church & State, Never
    the Twain Shall Meet?..................25
Chapter Three: Politics & Religion – Two
    Things We "Should Not Discuss"..................29
Chapter Four: Policy, Personality, Principle,
    and Political Platforms..................33
Chapter Five: Christian Nationalism and
    Other Straw Men..................37
Chapter Six: Fear of Imputed Racism..................41
Chapter Seven: The Kingdom of God: Past,
    Present, and Future..................45

Part Two: The Fruits of Fear..................49
Chapter Eight: What Happens When the
    Church is Silent on Morality..................51
Conclusion to Part Two: Fruit That Will Remain..................71

Appendix..................73
Discussion Questions:..................87
About the Author:..................91
End Notes..................95
Recommended Reading..................97

Foreword

Throughout my travels and ministry, I have observed a troubling reality: far too few ministers of the Gospel are willing to confront the perilous trends sweeping through our culture and even the Church, with the compassion and courage of a true "watchman on the wall." Christendom today is gripped by a profound spiritual lethargy, the very condition that may pave the way for the "great falling away" prophesied in 2 Thessalonians 2:1-3. In such perilous times however, God never leaves His people without hope. He sovereignly raises a standard, amplifying the voices of faithful watchmen to awaken His Bride and call her to revival.

Pastor Joel Rissinger is unmistakably one of those God-ordained voices. With rare wisdom, deep biblical knowledge, and unflinching spiritual insight, he sounds the alarm while extending grace and encouragement. He deserves our profound admiration and respect as a faithful watchman in this critical hour.

In an era marked by growing disunity within the Body of Christ and the proliferation of divisive, syncretic, and watered-down messages from far too many pulpits, Pastor Joel's latest book, *Pastors, Politics & Paranoia: Putting an End to the Crisis of Silence*, is nothing less than essential reading. This timely and illuminating work exposes how the Church has too often been silenced by intimidation, rendered complacent by comfort, and, through lack of biblical knowledge, made complicit in many of the evils advancing around us. With clarity and conviction, Pastor Joel exhorts us to break these cycles of "tolerant complacency," seize the power and anointing promised by the Holy Spirit, and position the Church for maximum Kingdom impact amid the present darkness spreading across the globe.

Pastors, Politics & Paranoia offers compelling, deeply researched insight into the myriad challenges confronting Christianity today. It shines a piercing light on the issues that have produced a spiritual malaise, causing many believers and leaders to hesitate in boldly upholding biblical truth in every sphere of life: family, education, government/politics, media, and culture. The crisis of silence, and in some cases outright complicity, in the face of grotesque global evils has undermined the Church's authority and effectiveness, reducing what should be a mighty force to a state of relative impotence. Pastor Joel accurately diagnoses these problems, pinpoints the critical domains where compromise has taken root, and provides practical, Spirit-led remedies that can revive, restore, and release fresh potency to both the Word of God and the Body of Christ.

At its core, this book serves as a profound wake-up call, a requiem for apathy, and a rallying cry for renewed zeal.

It equips readers with astute, concise biblical exposition alongside clear, actionable protocols for overcoming silence, fear, and complicity. Whether you are a pastor seeking courage to lead with boldness, or a parishioner longing to stand unashamedly for truth, this comprehensive resource will strengthen and mobilize you.

Having known Pastor Joel Rissinger personally for many years, I can testify that this book reflects the authentic heartbeat of a man consumed with zeal for God's glory and unwavering commitment to his calling as a watchman and disciple of Jesus Christ. His passion is contagious, his discernment sharp, and his love for the Church evident on every page.

Pastors, Politics & Paranoia is, without question, a must-read for every believer determined to resist the treacherous tides of cultural decay and the corrosive trends ushering in this era of present darkness. May it ignite a fresh fire in your soul and propel you to take your place on the wall.

In His service,

Dr. Kevin McGary
Author, Commentator, and President of Every Black Life Matters.

Introduction

Over the last 35 years of my ministry, I've watched pastors—myself included— grow timid about discussing some of the most pressing moral and cultural issues of our age. The moment a topic like abortion, marriage, sexuality, open borders, or law and order is raised, many church leaders retreat. Why? Because they're terrified of being branded "too political." Fears of driving new people away, alienating long-time members, losing 501c3 status, or even risking time in jail, keep pastors muzzled—and tragically, they've allowed secular voices to define what's right and wrong for an entire generation.

This must stop.

We're living through a moment that shakes the very core of what the American church is supposed to be. As I write this, the world reels from the assassination of Charlie Kirk. I have never seen so many professing Christians drawn together across borders and backgrounds, rallying around gospel hope in the wake of such tragedy. The Word of God rang loud, even from the lips of political leaders at a memorial that was broadcast to millions. Sadly, while many, if not most, Americans grieved Charlie's death, many did not. And, many of the most shocking voices of dissent didn't come just from outside the church—they came from within. I've watched with sadness and, at times, anger as pastors I respect, refused to discuss the murder, or worse, distanced themselves from Charlie as though his politics somehow nullified his faith.

Is it any wonder that millions of Christians don't vote—or vote for policies directly at odds with the teachings of Christ? We who are leaders in the modern church are responsible. Our silence has become complicity. Worse, some have twisted or watered down the faith, waving rainbow flags and preaching a watered-down gospel that never mentions repentance or obedience. In doing so, we risk the very crisis Jesus warned about in Matthew—many claiming to be His, but ultimately being rejected because the substance of gospel living was absent (Matthew 7:21–23).

This work is my modest attempt to break the silence. First, I'll address the roots of the fear and paranoia that have led so many pastors to tiptoe around the truth. Then, I'll examine the bitter fruit of this fear—a society adrift, cut loose from biblical moorings. My hope is not to end disagreement or controversy, but to invite real dialogue—and, perhaps, to inspire the courage that has always marked the church at her best.

Part One:
The Foundation of Fear

Chapter One

What ARE We Afraid Of?

A few years ago, I was having dinner with the President of the Zambian Wesleyan denomination near Livingston, Zambia, Bishop Juden Siachitema. He was also a Vice President of the Zambian Council of Churches at that time. As we devoured a traditional meal of Nshima and chicken stew, he leaned across the table and said, "Pastor Joel…what <u>are</u> you doing over there?!"

I knew what he meant. As a well-educated and well-informed leader, he had watched recent developments in American politics as well as the views and actions of the American church. I knew he was a conservative believer, a true man of God. So I swallowed hard, prayed a quick prayer, and responded. "Well, Bishop, we've lost our moorings. We're swimming in Jello. We've tossed aside our Constitution and worse, we've tossed aside our Bibles." His eyebrows furrowed, and he looked even more serious as I paused. "But

I want to assure you of something, Bishop," I continued, "When I speak to your pastors and leaders, the first thing I tell them is that they should NOT listen to us. 'Listen to Jesus,' I say, 'listen to the Apostles, pay attention to the scriptures. If what we teach is from the Bible, fine. But don't just listen to American preachers because we have nice clothes or money... listen to God.'"

"Very Good," the Bishop responded…"Very Good."

It's sad that I had to make this point, but it needed to be said. And while false gospel narratives abound, I would argue that the biggest reason for the decline of American Christianity isn't false teaching…

It's fear!

Scripture brims with commands about fear—or, rather, the rejection of it. "Perfect love casts out fear," John reminds us (1 John 4:18). Paul declares to Timothy, "God gave us a spirit not of fear but of power and love and self-control" (2 Timothy 1:7). Jesus said again and again, "Do not be afraid."

And yet, the reality is, in American pulpits it is unmistakable…we are afraid. The question begs to be asked—afraid of what, exactly?

First and most commonly, pastors confess they're afraid of losing people. The fear isn't always about losing newcomers, visitors, or antagonists and troublemakers—sometimes it's about losing good people, families who have been around for decades. Address a hot-button issue like abortion or same-sex marriage, and you risk seeing faithful attendees desert the pews, leaving behind a financial and relational crater.

Some hope that, if controversial topics are avoided, people will stick around long enough to "catch on" and eventually form biblical convictions. "Let's just preach Jesus," they argue. But does that really mean avoiding what Jesus Himself said/taught about marriage, sexuality, and the sanctity of life? And what is the gospel anyway—just a 30 second "elevator pitch" that omits any of Christ's teachings about life, morality, social justice, sex, or finances? Or is it much bigger than that, such that remaining silent on these things is to avoid preaching the good news as Christ intended? Silence, in that case, isn't "golden."

My experience tells me that if a pastor speaks boldly about what some consider a "controversial" topic some <u>may</u> leave. Still, I've found that others will <u>come</u> and stay because they appreciate the direct biblical teaching shared. Furthermore, when pastors avoid these topics, the result is quite different than what many leaders hope for. They hope that people will stay in the church long enough to get saved, read their Bibles, and discover the truth about the topics the pastor avoids bringing up in a public sermon. In fact, most people don't discover the truth about controversial topics because they're not studying the Word of God at a deep enough level. And, for those who DO "figure it out," they are often offended that this information wasn't given to them sooner. Thus, they may still leave, even if they had been in fellowship for months prior to their self-discovery. Furthermore, recent events suggest that those under 40 prefer a straight-forward, almost blunt sharing of the truth and find anything else unacceptable, fake, and even fraudulent.

While some pastors fear the loss of members/attenders, others fear governmental reprisal—the dreaded loss of nonprofit status, lawsuits, or public shaming. While such fears are rarely justified by precedent (liberal churches frequently endorse politicians or have them speak at church services with no consequence), the myth persists. "We can't talk about this…" they exclaim, "…or the IRS will come for us." Again, the result is silence.

Still others, perhaps unconsciously, imagine Jesus Himself standing in judgment of "conservative" stances, as if the Christ who called out sin with compassion and clarity, is now embarrassed by anyone who speaks hard truths in love. They fear being labeled unloving or cruel, despite the fact that coddling sin is never described as *love* in scripture.

But if we trace all of these anxieties to their source, we run into one primary culprit: a loss of the fear of God. When the church edits the gospel to avoid controversy, we're not protecting the faith—we're gutting it. We're fearing men over

God. Jesus's gospel was never meant to be reduced to a sound bite or a bumper-sticker slogan; it encompasses everything He taught, including all the uncomfortable, disruptive, and culturally unpopular bits. When we select only the pleasant verses and sidestep the tough stuff, we cease to preach the full counsel of God—and that, more than the disapproval of men, ought to make us tremble.

John Bevere, in his book, *The Awe of God*, argues powerfully that the church has traded holy fear for cultural conformity—a slow boil, nearly unnoticeable, yet deadly. The antidote is found not in timidity, but in repentance and a renewed respect for God's voice, whatever the personal cost.

Chapter Two

Church & State, Never the Twain Shall Meet?

Dr. Neil Anderson, in his famous "Steps to Freedom in Christ" process, teaches that irrational fear is based on lies we believe." In these next few chapters, we'll explore the untruths, half-truths, and irrational arguments that are often the basis for our irrational fear of preaching/teaching the whole counsel of scripture. One of the most common lies is the supposed definition and false implementation of our constitutional separation of church and state.

Let's be honest: The church in America, our media, and the federal government have turned "separation of church and state" into a muzzle. We tiptoe, worried we'll run afoul of an imaginary boundary, as if our calling was meant to stop at the sanctuary door. The first Christians understood no such line. Their faith shaped every inch of their lives and made waves in the public square—even when the cost was high (Acts 5:27–29).[1]

How did we get here? The founders' intent as seen in historical documents and memoirs, wasn't for faith to be stripped from public life. They wanted to guarantee religious freedom, not forbid religious conviction or action. In fact, the American Revolution was, in some ways, a revolt against the tyranny of a state-church, unmoored from the gospel. That's why many of those early patriots were ministers with muskets and pulpits—preaching that "resistance to tyranny is obedience to God."[2]

Making sure that faith was not controlled by the state was a priority for our founders. The Church of England, long influenced and controlled by the monarchy, was the antithesis of what they wanted for America. The church needed to be separate in order to influence the state and its leaders. It did not need to be silent or absent entirely, just free from political control so that if WOULDN'T be silent or emasculated.

Modern America, by contrast, flinches at the very odor of spiritual conviction in politics, as if faith corrupts public virtue, or violates some sacred code. Yet even our currency proclaims, "In God We Trust." Our courts demand witnesses swear to be truthful, "…so help me God." These are not the trappings of an atheistic republic, but signs of a people who once feared God and saw His truth as society's backbone.

We have let the culture define the debate—painting the church's moral witness as "imposing beliefs," while letting secularists frame the nation's moral dilemmas unchallenged. The result? Pastors avoid or apologize for biblical convictions, hoping to escape controversy, and secularists create rules promoting things like men using women's locker rooms to shower and change. What a tragedy! When the world needs the prophetic voice of the "city on a hill," we've given it confused psychobabble or awkward silence (Matthew 5:14). [3]

We claim believers cannot be involved in shaping public discourse, but that wasn't the mind of Christ, or the record of church history. From Wilberforce's abolition of the slave trade[4] to Dietrich Bonhoeffer's resistance against Nazi tyranny,[5] the gospel has always been a force for moral reform in the public forum—not through coercion, but through courageous witness.

I've seen, firsthand, what happens when pastors refuse to wall themselves off. By God's grace, my own ministry has allowed me to open public meetings in prayer or even serve as pastor or chaplain to city officials. This would have been impossible if I'd let this false "separation" gag my faith. I've had the blessing of giving prayerful support and even counsel to mayors, police chiefs, State House Representatives, governors, Chamber of Commerce and Rotary members, etc. It is only when believers lean in, not out, that we become salt and light. Furthermore, if we disconnect and remain silent, we have no right to complain or stand in judgement of those who are in charge and the sometimes-wretched policies they enact. Yes, it is much better to light a candle instead of cursing the darkness!

As biblical Christians, we don't want the state controlled by the church such that people are forced to be Christians (as if that were even possible). However, we DO want the freedom to influence and speak into the ears of our leaders for moral, gospel-focused, biblical clarity. If that's our heart and the focus of our teaching, constitutionally and legally, we have nothing to fear.

Chapter Three

Politics & Religion — Two Things We "Should Not Discuss?"

We've all heard it: "At dinner parties, we don't discuss politics or religion." But what most people call "good manners," is really just fear dressed up for company. And the truth is, the issues we're forbidden from discussing are exactly the issues most desperately in need of thoughtful, faithful conversation. An offshoot of the church and state fallacy, banning politics or religion from civil conversation is a deception that keeps us from solving some of our biggest problems.

When I have co-hosted radio programs in the past—one on a secular Hartford, Connecticut, station and another on a Christian network—I saw firsthand that people are hungry, not only for truth, but for a way to talk about it civilly. Despite being in the supposed "liberal wasteland" of Connecticut, people tuned in, called in, discussed, and debated some pretty conservative ideas introduced by the host. Why? Because when conversations are ground-ruled by mutual respect—no yelling, no name-calling, no ruses—real dialogue happens.

We had rules we enforced with the help of our producers and call screeners. We didn't allow callers to impute motives, call names, or curse. We didn't allow them to interrupt nor did we interrupt them. They had to tell our screeners why they were calling and then focus on that topic instead of blindsiding us with something else and then ranting on the air. By following these simple guidelines, we found we could talk about almost anything and actually learn from each other.

This isn't nostalgia; it's obedience to the biblical call for peace, patience, and gentleness (2 Timothy 2:24–26[6]). The biblical preachers of the gospel never shied away from controversy, but they did set a standard for how controversies are handled: "speaking the truth in love" (Ephesians 4:15), and as Paul writes, "let your gentleness be evident to all" (Philippians 4:5).

What's gotten lost? We prefer comfort to clarity, and false unity over truth. Yet, silence isn't really neutral. It's surrender, and often it's viewed as tacit approval. Refusing to speak means letting the loudest, least biblical voices frame every hot-button issue—from the sanctity of life and marriage, to economics and justice.

Worse, this silence splinters the Christian life. If we

can't talk about politics and faith honestly, then faith is quarantined to Sunday, and the rest of life is run by a different set of values. James warns against this double-mindedness (James 1:8). Christ does not allow us to don "secular hats" and "sacred hats." He calls us to a whole-life obedience (Colossians 3:17).

Is it any wonder that politicians can call themselves "Christian" while supporting policies that offend every Christian tenet? Could it be that our inability to have reasonable discussions about things like politics or our faith has led us to have political leaders who claim to be Christians, while voting to support abortion on demand, transgender education in our schools, allowing men in women's locker rooms, same-sex marriages, and other abominations?

When pressed on some of these things, leaders will suggest that their faith is separate from their civic duty as a congressman or even as a president. Is this what Jesus intends—that we segment our lives such that we can, in Jekyll-and-Hyde-like fashion, support a moral duplicity that leads to a corrupt and collapsing culture?? Did our founding fathers here in the US intend that our faith never influence public policy?

Of course not!

I'm recommending a return to civil discourse with similar house rules to what we used on the radio. I believe that when these rules are followed and people replace unbridled emotion with logic and reason, agreement is often attainable. Furthermore, when we must "agree to disagree," there is still an opportunity to improve understanding between people at opposite ends of the political or religious spectrum. Is this possible with everyone? No. Some will have to be banned from the discussion for not following the rules. Still, those who are left may benefit immensely from discussing the things "we're not supposed to talk about." Frankly, since I believe the Bible is inerrant and inspired by God, a civil conversation rooted in Biblical fact normally leads to agreement based on truth.

Sadly, when we avoid this kind of dialogue, we reap the consequences of our compartmentalized faith: compromise, confusion, and, ultimately, societal collapse. We must recover the art of civil discourse, rooted in truth and love. Jesus Himself sparred with Pharisees and reasoned with crowds, but He did so with a clarity and compassion that changed hearts (Matthew 22:15–22). If we stop talking, we yield the field—and watch as error takes root.

Chapter Four

Policy, Personality, Principle, and Political Platforms

Here's the hard truth: The Christian vote in America is often swayed neither by policy nor principle, but by personality, party loyalty, or even media-driven optics. I have asked countless believers: "Can you name one DNC platform point in the last two elections that aligns with Scripture?" When I do this, the room normally goes silent. Not one example is given. Instead, I hear about Trump's tweets or a liberal socialist candidate's "niceness." It's as if, when voting, Christians are guided by the fruit of an ad campaign, rather than the root of sound policy.

This is not how God calls us to discernment. Jesus said, "Do not judge by appearances, but judge with right judgment" (John 7:24). The prophet Samuel nearly made the same mistake, looking at Eliab's looks rather than David's heart

(1 Samuel 16:7). God's criteria cut deeper: Righteousness, justice, mercy, truth (Micah 6:8).

Do I excuse candidates who lack character? No—wickedness in personal life is serious. But when the ballot is cast, it must be cast by the light of principle and policy over party, politics, personality, or personal preferences. When the early church weighed leadership, character mattered, but so did doctrine and faithfulness (1 Timothy 3:1–13). Likewise, our votes must prioritize what leaders do, and what they stand for, over slick presentations or personal charisma.

Believe me, I'm not a party hack. Over the years, I've voted for Republicans, Democrats, and Independents—based on which candidate's platform best aligned, even imperfectly, with the biblical convictions I hold. Let me say plainly: If Christians had voted the teaching of Scripture over the past 15 years, many "progressive" policies we now suffer with, would never have survived. Christian apathy or confusion is the reason policies like abortion-on-demand, transgender experiments on children, and assaults on marriage law have gained steam. Since census data suggests that over 62% of adults identify as Christian, their votes should have prohibited such policies from being established. Sadly, this didn't happen.

Christians are not called to ignorance or passivity. God says, "My people perish for lack of knowledge" (Hosea 4:6). If "we the people" are the authority in our form of government, and we are to work with and submit to that government (Romans 13), then to abdicate informed civic stewardship is both unbiblical and un-American.

So, what, then, is the way forward?

Pastors, it's time to "preach the word in season and out of season" (2 Tim. 4:2), especially on issues where Scripture is clear. The sanctity of life. The necessity of protecting the innocent. The value of boundaries—both personal and national (Proverbs 22:28). The meaning of marriage (Genesis 2:24, Ephesians 5:31–32). The bedrock of justice and mercy in public life (Micah 6:8).

If we teach these first principles, we give the church a lodestar in the fog. Christians, educated in the Word, can apply wisdom to the ballot box and the public square—not as theocratic bullies, but as citizens faithful to both gospel and country.

Would this reshape America's politics? You'd better believe it! But the goal isn't a "Christian party"—it's a consistently Christian people, judging policy by principle, and principle by the Word of God.

Chapter Five

Christian Nationalism and Other Straw Men

One of the most effective weapons used to silence the modern church is the term "Christian Nationalism." The accusation of being a "Christian Nationalist" isn't even subtle anymore—stand for biblical convictions in the public arena, and suddenly you're branded an extremist, a theocrat, or worse. This label, tossed out by academics and activists, is meant to shame Christians into retreating from public influence as if the simple claim that faith shapes citizenship is in itself, dangerous.

Let's get real: "Christian Nationalism," as commonly painted, is mostly a scarecrow, a straw man. Critics say it's the sinister fusion of faith and flag, the conflation of patriotism and piety, and the attempt to forcibly impose religious law on a pluralistic nation. But here's the truth—most Christians participating in public life aren't advocating for theocracy, but simply to refuse to check their deepest convictions at the voting booth door (or curtain). And why should they? Our founders didn't want the state to control faith, but neither did they want the faithful forbidden from shaping civic virtue.

The "strange new fire" against Christian engagement isn't just unfair, it's historically illiterate. Christians shaped the West's moral sensibilities on everything from slavery to civil rights precisely because their faith compelled public witness. "Let your light shine before others, so that they may see your good works and give glory to your Father in heaven," Jesus said (Matthew 5:16). That's not a call for totalitarianism, but to visible integrity—in every area of life, including politics.

Do some cross the line into syncretism, wrapping Christianity in national colors and confusing the gospel with party platforms? Sure, and that deserves rebuke. Idolatry of nation is as offensive as idolizing wealth or fame (Deuteronomy 6:14–15). But most believers aren't guilty of this. They simply want a nation governed by justice, mercy, and truth, which is the law God wrote on the human heart (Romans 2:15).

So, when critics use "Christian Nationalism" as a sledgehammer to attack any biblical witness in public debate, remember: That attack tells you more about their view of faith than about the actual convictions of millions of believers. We are not called to be theocrats, but neither are we called to be cowards.

The real danger here is not a Christian takeover, but a Christian silence—ceding the ground so thoroughly that truth itself is labeled hate speech and virtue is treated as vice. "Woe to those who call evil good and good evil," Isaiah warned (Isaiah 5:20). The church must not let itself be caricatured into irrelevance.

Now I recognize that many evangelicals will point to John's prophetic warnings in Revelation regarding the woman who rides the beast and a future church-state empire which will do harm, even killing believers (Revelation 17). To avoid misinterpretation or misapplication, we must remember a few facts about this prophecy:

1. The woman in Revelation 17 is not the true church. She is corrupt—referred to as a prostitute, not a group of true believers. Looking at the current world religious climate, it's doubtful that the "Woman" is even a nominally Christian entity. Thus, the fruit of the woman's influence is evil, not good. This is a very different outcome than what we've seen historically when the church takes her rightful role as a healthy influencer of political powers.

2. Again, Revelation seems to foretell a church-state combination, not a healthy separation such as we've been discussing in this book. The woman isn't just advising the government, she's apparently controlling it. This is not what I, nor others of like mind, are calling for.

Straw men—bogus supposed "threats" promoted as warnings by a culture desiring to keep the church locked away in irrelevancy—should never stop our witness. We are needed by a dark and dying world because of the light of truth we possess. Christian Nationalism is the most prominent of these, but others exist as well. Christians fear being called "right-wing extremist," "cult-like," "overly fundamentalist," "exclusive," and many other things. I suggest we simply promote ourselves as biblical Christ followers. If other labels come our way, we must lovingly, but firmly dismiss them and keep teaching the truth.

Chapter Six

Fear of Imputed Racism

There's another potent specter stalking the pulpit—the fear of being called a racist. In a culture hypersensitive to any perceived slight, many pastors grow timid lest they offend, or worse, be accused of bigotry when confronting topics like law and order, immigration, socialism, or biblical teaching on sexuality. No matter how faithfully you preach, the threat formula lingers: "If you say X, someone will accuse you of not being sensitive to Y."

Let me be frank. Racism is a sin. Discrimination and ethnic hatred grieve the heart of God, who "from one man made every nation of mankind" (Acts 17:26). The cross of Christ obliterates all dividing walls (Ephesians 2:14–16). The American church has much to repent over regarding racial injustice in the past, and if she does not, Jesus will judge her for it. But standing for scripture on moral issues isn't bigotry. Not every application of biblical conviction is a veiled attack on minority groups—though in the modern dialect, that accusation comes fast, hot, and often as a power play more than a plea for justice.

Preaching truth about borders, criminality, work ethic, traditional family structures, or sexual ethics doesn't have to come with hatred or insensitivity. Paul commands us to "Speak the truth in love," (Ephesians 4:15). Thus, it can and must be done. The law of God applies impartially: "You shall do no injustice in court. You shall not be partial to the poor or defer to the great, but in righteousness shall you judge your neighbor" (Leviticus 19:15).

Courageous, Christ-centered preaching will bother both racist bigots and virtue-signaling ideologues. If you proclaim biblical equity—true impartiality—prepare to be misunderstood on both sides. Jesus Himself was denounced by Pharisees and Sadducees, called a drunk and a glutton, slandered with every insult at their disposal (Luke 7:34).

But Pastors, we cannot let the fear of slander freeze us into silence. If your conscience is clear, your heart obedient, and your tone is one of kingdom love, endure the name-calling. "Blessed are you when others revile you…on my account" (Matthew 5:11). The real tragedy is when fear shuts our mouths, and the culture is discipled by anyone but the church.

And, there's good news here as well. As mentioned earlier, there are people—thousands of them—waiting for pastors and teachers who will boldly stand-up to these attacks and preach the truth. A careful study of church growth over the past decade indicates a shift toward those who use their pulpits to preach the whole counsel of scripture, even when it's not culturally WOKE or popular. Could you actually see growth by taking a public stand against evil? Yes…yes you could, if it's done boldly and in love.

The experience around Turning Point USA and the martyrdom of Charlie Kirk is a great example of this. Some pastors avoided talking about Charlie's assassination because they had heard accusations of racism involving Charlie's comments about Dr. Martin Luther King. One of my friends, a friend of Charlie's, Dr. Kevin McGary, a black commentator and author, as President of Every Black Life Matters, has addressed this. Kevin says, "Charlie's comments about Dr. King had to do with King's well-known adultery and sexual misconduct, even during the week of his murder. Charlie's position was that this made Dr. King a poor role model for young men in general. This had nothing to do with the fact that Dr. King was black."

Still, hearing that some accused Charlie Kirk of racism, several pastors avoided talking about him from the pulpit. Shame! How much better would it be to address the facts, including the fact that many black men such as Dr McGary support Charlie as anything but racist in his views?

If we are truly color blind as a nation, speaking out

against the views or behavior of someone who happens to be of a different skin tone, should never be a basis for labeling that speaker as racist. We witnessed the antithesis of this during President Barak Obama's presidency where to question his positions on virtually any topic landed you in the racial "basket of deplorables," as Hilary Clinton labeled it. We speak the truth in love and, while we should never let racial bias enter our preaching, the fear of it shouldn't render us silent either.

Chapter Seven

The Kingdom of God: Past, Present, and Future

To reckon with these fears, we must return to the supreme vision—the Kingdom of God. Jesus didn't launch His mission with a political manifesto. He began with a bold declaration: "Repent, for the kingdom of heaven is at hand" (Matthew 4:17). His authority was never borrowed from Caesar or Pilate, nor was it limited to a future heaven. Christ's kingdom is both already and not yet—past, present, and future breaking into the world.

The Kingdom of God is not America, nor any other secular nation. It's a spiritual reality with social and cultural implications for all mankind. Christ's reign affects all spheres—private and public, individual and corporate. Our loyalty is first to Him, which then flows out in prophetic love and public witness.

As the church, we're called to bear witness to a kingdom that challenges every earthly regime. We are "aliens and strangers" (1 Peter 2:11), yet commanded to "seek the welfare of the city" (Jeremiah 29:7). Our citizenship is in heaven (Philippians 3:20), but our presence is for the good of the world. We do not preach policy for its own sake, but to proclaim Christ's lordship over every inch of creation (Colossians 1:16–18).

The church must not pin her hope to any political throne. Yet she must not hide in irrelevant piety, forgetting her prophetic charge. The world needs the Kingdom—bursting forth in churches that are bold, loving, wise, and courageous. Anything less is not the gospel of Jesus.

I believe we witnessed an excellent example of this during the memorial service for Charlie Kirk. Political leaders at the very top of our republic shared clear presentations of the gospel and gave witness of their own faith and Charlie's impact on them. As a believer, I found it hard to hold back tears as I watched along with millions of others. Did these men suggest that they saw the United States government as the incarnation of Christ's Kingdom? No! Rather, they talked about how their role in this government has been impacted by their faith—just as Charlie Kirk's political positions were based on his. This is the balance—this is the goal. This is what we must strive for.

PART TWO:
The Fruits of Fear

Note: In this next section, we will explore the results of letting fear control our witness and our teaching. The goal isn't to accuse, but to illustrate and inspire change....

Chapter Eight

What Happens When the Church Is Silent on Morality

Our silence isn't just an offense to the holy calling of the pulpit. It is, more gravely, an aid to darkness. Where the church mutes God's truth, culture is catechized by media, entertainment, and the latest activist cause. Moral confusion sweeps in—on sexuality, the meaning of marriage, the value of life, and the dignity of work—because the lighthouse (the church) flickers, then fades.

History offers warnings about this. When ancient Israel turned from God, "Everyone did what was right in his own eyes" (Judges 21:25). In the silence of the prophets, kings and priests alike fell into compromise and decay. When Wilberforce started campaigning against the slave trade, the official church mostly shrugged. When Bonhoeffer began to denounce Hitler's Reich, most German pastors went silent, and the price was catastrophe. Silence is never neutral.

In today's America, surveys show that even basic Christian confession—like the deity of Christ or the authority of scripture—has eroded among self-identified evangelicals. [7] Why? Because the groundwork of clear teaching has been neglected in a generation raised on "safe" sermons and inoffensive spirituality. The result: a church ashamed of the gospel (Romans 1:16), and a nation losing its moral compass.

Our Lord called us to be salt—preserving what is good and prophetic. When we lose our distinctiveness ("if the salt loses its saltiness…"), we are, in Jesus' own words, "no longer good for anything, except to be thrown out and trampled underfoot" (Matthew 5:13).

If the church will not courageously speak on abortion, marriage, family, or justice, someone else will fill the void— and their vision will not be God's. Preaching on morality isn't a bonus round—it's a life-or-death duty.

Let's explore many of these culturally "hot-button" topics briefly from a biblical and historical perspective:

*Abortion & The Sanctity of Life

The silence of the church on abortion has had devastating consequences. The numbers themselves are staggering: since Roe v. Wade (1973), over 60 million unborn children have been lost to abortion in America alone. But the cost isn't only counted in lives ended—it's measured in consciences dulled, moral spheres emptied, and churches that traded holiness for peace at any price.

How did it happen? The pulpits grew quiet. Pastors worried about seeming "political," while politicians and the media seized the language: "choice," "reproductive justice," "women's healthcare." The vocabulary of termination was sanitized and stripped of consequence. Rarely do we hear the sanctity of unborn life described in the simple, honest terms Scripture uses: "You knit me together in my mother's womb... I am fearfully and wonderfully made" (Psalm 139:13–14), a child, not a "problem" or a "potential."

And so, generations have come to believe that morality is up for debate, or worse—that it can be legislated out of existence. When pastors avoid the hard questions, abortion isn't de-escalated as a theological or personal crisis. Instead, it is reframed as a private choice, no more morally weighty than picking out wallpaper.

But the Bible is not silent. Both Old and New Testament speak to God's extraordinary care for the vulnerable. "Do not shed innocent blood" was not only a commandment (Jeremiah 22:3), but breaking it invited national judgment (2 Kings 24:4). Jesus himself, blessing infants and warning that God cares for even the "least of these," leaves no doubt about His stance (Matthew 18:1–6).

Our culture will answer for this. But judgment begins with the house of God (1 Peter 4:17). When pastors refuse to defend the unborn, they not only fail the children, but also abandon scared mothers, confused fathers, and entire communities in desperate need of healing and truth. The gospel offers forgiveness, but also the charge: "Go, and sin no more" (John 8:11). Silence signals surrender—not just of an issue, but of a calling.

What would renewal look like? It would mean preaching compassion and courage together: hating sin, not the sinner. Offering practical care for women in crisis—adoption, shelter, material support. Daring to speak what is true and costly, just as the first Christians did when Roman culture discarded its unwanted children on the city dump. Christianity changed the world once on this very point. It can do so again if we will open our lips.

*Marriage

Marriage is no small detail in the biblical story—it's woven into the very fabric of creation. "A man shall leave his father and mother and be joined to his wife, and they shall become one flesh" (Genesis 2:24). This is not social convention, but divine decree, repeated by Jesus himself (Matthew 19:4–6).

Yet today, marriage means almost anything—or nothing at all. Years of pulpit silence have allowed every cultural innovation to take root: easy divorce, trivial "hook-up culture," same-sex marriage, and the redefining of husband, wife, and family altogether. Some even promote bestiality or incest as acceptable sexual behaviors in our modern context.

When pastors flinch before the world's definitions, they are not showing compassion. They are abandoning biblical truth at the moment it's most needed. Even as courts and legislatures redrew the lines, too many church leaders adopted the world's vocabulary: "love is love," or, "marriage equality." The Scripture's countercultural call was muted, and a generation was left to believe that God's design was at best outdated, at worst oppressive.

But Scripture remains, stubborn and lovingly clear. Marriage is a living picture of Christ and His church (Ephesians 5:31–32). It's meant to be lifelong, unifying, sexually exclusive, and generative—open to children and to the self-giving love God intended from the beginning. To shrink from teaching this out of fear of controversy or being labeled "out of touch"—is to fail in shepherding.

Our refusal to speak up on marriage doesn't keep the peace; it sows confusion. Children hunger for stability, love, and the security that comes from parents united in truth. Broken marriages cascade across generations, and society pays a steep price: fatherlessness, poverty, crime. Perhaps the most devasting fruit of our silence is the national divorce rate of over 50% and the frivolous approach to divorce and remarriage in the modern church. Instead of looking at Jesus' teaching in Matthew 19 and Paul's added clarity in I Corinthians 7, the church has promoted easy divorce and unquestioned remarriage such that our ability to uphold scriptural views on marriage in general is duplicitous and weak.

The call, then, is not to rage against the world, but to model a new and better way. Husbands, love your wives as Christ loved the church (Ephesians 5:25). Wives, honor your husbands as to the Lord (Ephesians 5:22). Do these things generally with very few exceptions, "till death do us part." Pastors, teach these truths without apology—from the pulpit, in counseling, through church policy—and help nurture healthy, holy homes in a broken age.

*Human Sexuality & Transgender Ideation

No topic today is more charged—or more silenced by the church than sexuality and gender. The language shifts so fast that many Christians, unsure what to say, say nothing. Meanwhile, activists and school curricula claim authority: "Gender is a social construct," they proclaim, "Everyone has a right to define themselves," and now, "Children must be affirmed, not questioned, even in the matter of their bodies."

Before her retirement after spending decades as a School Psychologist, my wife was pressured to influence a young girl regarding her sexual identity. The eight-year-old girl was what we would have called a "tomboy." While loudly proclaiming herself as a girl, she loved boy's clothing and was proud of her ability to compete with elementary school boys on the playground. Sadly, woke school officials and even the girl's parents were pushing her to consider using the boys bathroom and start referring to herself as male. My wife, to her credit, did not go along with this and eventually, the pressure subsided. She later told me that had she not retired, she might have eventually been fired due to her unwillingness to support such gender dysphoric nonsense.

Beneath all the noise, Scripture still speaks. From the very beginning: "Male and female he created them" (Genesis 1:27). Sexual difference is not oppressive, but a gift, dignifying and distinct. Sex is not just about pleasure, but about love, covenant, and creative partnership in God's world. Teaching this and helping children who suffer from any gender confusion is an act of compassion, not hate.

Clearly our culture's confusion has real effects—on children medicated and mutilated before they can buy cigarettes, on families torn apart, on a nation called to celebrate what previous generations would have called a desperate need for help. The fruits of unhinged sexual liberation and gender denial have been devastation: higher rates of depression, suicide, and brokenness among those who believed a surgical answer could solve an existential ache.

Silence from pastors only feeds this confusion. We'd do well to remember what Paul taught the Church in sexually chaotic Corinth. "God is not a God of confusion, but of peace" (1 Corinthians 14:33). Failing to teach clearly—compassionately, yes, but unmistakably—leaves children prey to the culture's experimentation. Paul warned Timothy that in the last days, many would "turn away from listening to the truth and wander off into myths" (2 Timothy 4:4).

What's needed is neither cruelty nor acquiescence, but committed love that dares to speak God's design, offers support to the struggling, and refuses to surrender the next generation to an ever-changing ideological fog.

*Homosexuality & the LGBTQ++ Agenda

Few areas have seen cultural change as rapidly—or been as celebrated—as attitudes around homosexuality and the LGBTQ++ movement. Parades that began as calls for tolerance have become annual celebrations of sexual revolution. And all the while, the church has been pressured: stay silent, "be nice," or get called hateful and bigoted.

Let there be no mistake: every person bears dignity as an image-bearer of God (Genesis 1:26). We're called to love and welcome sinners—of every kind—without malice or mockery. Furthermore, sexual sin of any kind is no worse than sins such as lying, gossip, murder, or gluttony. But love never demands the abandonment of truth. Paul's words to the Corinthian church are as needed today as in the first century: "Do you not know that the unrighteous will not inherit the kingdom of God? Do not be deceived: neither the sexually immoral, nor idolaters, nor adulterers, nor men who practice homosexuality…" (1 Corinthians 6:9–11). The gospel offers hope, not justification for any sin.

The modern church faces an almost impossible challenge: how to speak a clear "no" to sin, while still demonstrating Christ's wide mercy. The answer: by pointing all—straight, gay, confused, searching—to the cross, where repentance and transformation are actually possible (2 Corinthians 5:17).

When we teach these things, do all gay Christians become straight? No, although I've known several who have. For many, same sex attraction is something they'll have their entire lives. Still, like their heterosexual counterparts who are single, they strive to remain celibate since it's not the attraction that constitutes sin, but rather the action of physically and/or mentally engaging in sex outside of the biblical marriage covenant. (I've often told over-zealous hetero men who proclaim that all "gays go to hell," that if being attracted to someone you're not married to meant a sure plummet to hell, every man I know is doomed!)

As we've stated, the cost of silence, or compromise, is high. Our witness suffers, and the world sees a faith too weak to stand for its own scripture, much less save. Let the story instead be one of both conviction and kindness—a church as clear as Christ, and as full of grace.

*Male and Female Roles

Today's culture rebels not just against distinctions in sexuality, but against God-ordained difference itself. The very ideas of "manhood" and "womanhood" are called oppressive, outdated, or even toxic. The Bible's teaching on gender roles is especially targeted: wives submitting to husbands, husbands laying down their lives. Yet God's ordering wasn't arbitrary—it was designed to display mutual glory and unique calling (Ephesians 5, Colossians 3).

When the church refuses to teach on these roles, we contribute to the crisis. Children lose models of sacrifice and love; spouses embark on marriage with no sense of their holy calling. Leadership—whether in the home or church—becomes unmoored from service and self-giving, and falls prey to the culture's confusion. I would argue that a certain measure of our cultures' gender dysphoria is due to egalitarian concepts promoted in some churches where men and women are to be seen as not just equal, but equivalent—non-distinct in every way. This is absurd, but it is common knowledge that men and women are unique not just physically but emotionally, mentally in terms of how we process information, and in many other ways as well.

Is the biblical vision of gender abused in the church? Sometimes. In the past, it has been twisted into bullying or passivity, manipulation or cowardice. But the answer to misuse isn't to mute the message; it's to recover its beauty. "In Christ there is neither Jew nor Greek, slave nor free, male nor female..." (Galatians 3:28), Paul declares—but this speaks not of role erasure, but of radical equality in worth and access to God. It's a spiritual equality. Paul can preach dignity while upholding difference. So must we. We simply need to remember that after creating man as both male and female, God proclaimed these differences "very good (Genesis 1:26–27)."

*Immigration

Immigration has become a flashpoint for American culture and, sadly, for the church—a subject increasingly shrouded in silence for fear of being called unloving, unwelcoming, or even xenophobic. Yet the Bible says much about foreigners, borders, law, and compassion.

Scripture is clear: "You shall treat the stranger who sojourns with you as the native among you, and you shall love him as yourself" (Leviticus 19:34). God's people are commanded to show kindness, hospitality, and respect to the outsider. Jesus Himself was a refugee child, fleeing Herod's violence (Matthew 2:13–15). But biblical compassion does not abolish the rule of law or erase national sovereignty. Even in ancient Israel, there were gates, boundaries, and laws for entry (Numbers 15:14–16). Even between tribes as part of the same nation, God required very specific, well documented boundaries (Joshua chapters 13–21).

Modern debate has turned these both/ands into either/ors: You're either for open borders and nationally-funded welfare for all, or you have no heart. That is a false dilemma. Healthy societies, like healthy families, set boundaries out of love— welcoming the guest, but doing so with order, accountability, and respect for justice. The Good Samaritan (Luke 10:25–37) saw a wounded neighbor and acted sacrificially, risking his own comfort. But he did not erase all distinctions, nor did he condone criminal trespassing or disregard for God's law. And what did the open border policy of the Biden era, supposedly a reflection of love and a respect for freedom, produce? Increased crime, child trafficking, drug abuse/smuggling, poverty, homelessness, and more....

The church's role must be to model real hospitality— supporting legal, orderly immigration, providing aid and friendship to newcomers, and advocating reform where laws are unjust. As someone married to an immigrant (as are our current President Donald Trump and Vice President J. D.

Vance), I value immigration. I just want it done right and with respect for the rule of law. I worked with my wife to obtain her legal citizenship so that she could vote, etc. While I saw the need for change in the process, I value going through it versus trying to cheat it or just ignore it as millions have done. To do it right, we must reject the fear-driven silence that hands complex questions to politicians or ideologues alone. When the church won't lead, others will fill the vacuum—with simplistic slogans, anger, or chaos.

One way the church can lead is in what I love to call holistic missions. During His earthly ministry, Jesus never went into a village and **only** preach to the people…nor did he go to a city and **only** feed them without sharing the gospel of the kingdom. He never healed the sick but left people hungry for spiritual or physical sustenance. For Jesus, missions was an all-encompassing package of physical and spiritual blessing. Further, the blessing was the truth which, if practiced, could lead to more blessing including the meeting of basic needs (see Matthew 6:33).

When we bless people in other countries, their need to flee to our country and illegally cross the border diminishes. One of the best examples of what I'm suggesting here is the Sons of Thunder Farm near Livingston, Zambia. Sons of Thunder teaches biblical farming techniques, provides medical care and a nationally-renowned birthing center, offers schools for children, and based on prolific gospel preaching has planted and supported numerous churches throughout the region. They've provided wells with fresh water, grain for the hungry, prayer and healing for the sick, and God's Word for all who will listen. I love to call it "one-stop shopping." To learn more, visit their website, https://www.sotministry.org/. If missions programs were less segmented and more integrated like this one, I believe the immigration crisis in many western countries would virtually disappear. People in villages all around the Sons of Thunder Farm are blessed and happy. Few would consider fleeing to the US and leaving their own beloved country.

Our message in brief: Boundaries are loving. Justice is loving. And so is kindness to the foreigner. Let's embrace a biblical both/and, confronting hard realities without losing our hearts.[8]

*Law & Order

Pastors today fear even mentioning "law and order"— not for lack of biblical warrant, but for dread of being misunderstood. Culture increasingly views police, courts, prisons, and enforcement itself with suspicion. Some of that suspicion is warranted. Injustice—racial profiling, brutality, corruption—grieves God. "Woe to those who acquit the guilty for a bribe and deprive the innocent of their rights!" (Isaiah 5:23). But the abuse of law is not an argument for lawlessness. Nor is having a position of legal authority an automatic indication of corruption.

Scripture is clear: God ordains governing authorities to "bear the sword" for good, punishing evil, and protecting the innocent (Romans 13:1–4). The psalmist prays for rulers "to judge your people with righteousness, and your poor with justice" (Psalm 72:2). To abolish order is not compassion; it is abdication. Solomon saw this: "When justice is done, it brings joy to the righteous but terror to evildoers" (Proverbs 21:15).

The present cultural moment tries to redefine all authority as oppressive, every boundary as harmful. Defunding police, decriminalizing vice, declaring "my truth" as a subjective reality with no objective truth/facts as foundational—these feed chaos, not peace. Some politicians promote the use of social workers in lieu of police. While social work has its place, sending an unarmed counselor into a domestic violence situation can be dangerous to all involved. Churches that will not speak clearly about justice and order send the message that the only sin left is to punish sin. This plays into the devil's plan to "kill and destroy" (John 10:10).

Is there a danger of idolizing the state? Yes. But there is an equal danger—one too often realized—of refusing to uphold God's expectation for righteous order, due process, and real consequences for evil. The church must resist both extremes. "Learn to do good; seek justice, correct oppression; bring justice to the fatherless, plead the widow's cause," Scripture commands (Isaiah 1:17). But always—always— within the context of moral order and law.

*Socialism, Communism, and Economic Equity

The rush of young Americans toward socialism and even communism has left many pastors shell-shocked. "Do I dare say from the pulpit that biblical justice is not the same as enforced income redistribution or state control of property?" some question. "Or will I be accused of hating the poor, or worse, of political extremism?" Silence, once again, becomes the easiest option.

Here, too, the Scripture is not bashful. From Genesis onward, private property is presumed: "You shall not steal" (Exodus 20:15); "Do not move your neighbor's boundary stone" (Deuteronomy 19:14). The early church's radical generosity—selling lands and sharing with any who had need (Acts 2:44–45)—was voluntary, Spirit-led, not by government edict. Paul rebukes those who "will not work," and says that if someone refuses to be productive, "let him not eat" (2 Thessalonians 3:10).

Does God care about structural oppression, just wages, and the fate of the poor? Deeply. "Whoever oppresses the poor taunts his Maker" (Proverbs 17:5). The prophets thundered against injustice and exploitation. But God's solution—generosity, fair treatment, community—never confused compassion with forced parity. Nowhere in the New Testament is government called to own the means of production or to dissolve the family's economic role.

The scripture also understands human nature in a way that communist or socialist leaders such as Marx never did/have. Jeremiah 17:9 tells us that the natural human heart is "desperately wicked and deceitful." For socialism to work, humans, especially government leaders, would need to be universally pure and unselfish in motive. The fact that we are not has proven scripture correct in that every attempt to implement these socialist governmental systems has failed throughout history.

The biblical vision is beautiful but challenging: radical voluntary giving (2 Corinthians 9:7), the dignity of work, stewardship as a trust before God, and justice that lifts the weak without crushing ambition or distorting the image of God in work and reward. Based on the "new heart" spiritually granted when a person embraces Christ unto salvation, people are able to live out these values where unbelievers cannot (Ezekiel 36:26, Hebrews 8, etc.).

The tragedy is, when pastors do not teach these things, young believers are discipled by the slogans on X, not the wisdom of Scripture. They are vulnerable to believing that socialism is "more Christian" because of a false promise of everyone being equal and will be given an equal share. They also fail to recognize that power-hungry, selfish leaders in countries that proclaim socialism as a virtuous system take most of the money, food, and other valuables for themselves, leaving the average person impoverished.

True equity isn't sameness—it's faithfulness and stewardship, thriving within God's good boundaries. It's time for the Church of Jesus Christ to loudly proclaim these things!

*The REAL Purpose of Human Government

Where cultural heat blazes, scriptural light must shine brightest. Why does government exist, according to the Bible? Not to replace family, church, or the accountability of individual conscience, but "to be God's servant for your good" (Romans 13:4).

Government's legitimate role is to reward the good, restrain the evil, administer justice, and protect the innocent. It cannot save souls, reorder hearts, or substitute human authority for divine. When government stays in its lane, it is a blessing—when it supplants God's order, it becomes cruel. See the warnings about kings in 1 Samuel 8:10–18, or Nebuchadnezzar's abuses in Daniel 3–6. Glorious nations have crumbled under the weight of bloated bureaucracy and tyranny.

Christians must beware of two equal and opposite errors: making government their "savior," expecting it to supply virtue, happiness, and every need; or making it their enemy, disengaging altogether. Both paths lead to disaster. Instead, we are called to honor, pray for, obey when we can, and stand courageously when we must. "We must obey God rather than men" (Acts 5:29). Good government is a gift. Idolatrous government is to be opposed.

Finally, American believers should take seriously the Romans 13 responsibility we all share. Since ours is a "government for the people, by the people," every believer IS a government official. At minimum, our votes are a part of exercising our God-given responsibility to ensure that WE the People govern based on truth and justice. We must pray, be active, and take that role seriously…which leads us to our next topic….

*Fair Elections

Our silence on elections is not a virtue but an abdication. Honest government cannot endure without trust. "Unequal weights and measures are an abomination to the Lord" (Proverbs 20:23). Voting fraud, manipulation, and corruption are not merely political issues—they are moral crises, striking at the heart of justice.

Churches, fearing charges of partisanship, often refuse to teach that the integrity of the process matters to God. Yet, nations survive or fall based on the honesty of their stewards (see Daniel 6:4, where Daniel's faithfulness set him apart even in a "hostile" regime). Advocating for secure and transparent elections is not idolatry of democracy—it's love of neighbor and commitment to righteousness.

Of course, this starts with pastors encouraging Christians to vote and take part in the democratic process themselves. Many have become proud of the fact that they do not and yet, when evil leaders are put in place, they complain and rant. Again, I believe that in a Representative Republic like the US, Romans 13 would have us recognize that we ARE the government and thus have an obligation to exercise our authority in the voting booth. Since many don't, or only do so haphazardly, it's no wonder we are silent and absent from the fight for fair elections.

Our great temptation is to despise elections as hopelessly rigged or to enshrine them as sacrosanct. Both errors betray a lack of faith. Instead, our calling is to pursue what is right, teach what is true, and call all to account—ourselves, rulers, and processes alike. A nation that cannot trust its systems will, eventually, descend into chaos or tyranny. The church must not shrink from telling this truth.

I also recognize that many of my Calvinist brothers believe that the outcome of all elections is predetermined by God. My Arminian Theology overflows with counter arguments concerning this view, but I think we should all be able to agree on one basic principle: God would most likely prefer to fulfill his will regarding our leaders by using us as His servants instead of having us absent from the process, opposing the process, or allowing the process to be corrupt. Thus, we have a call to work together for good when it comes to electoral integrity.

Conclusion to Part Two

Fruit That Will Remain

What you see in America today, in every domain listed above, is not merely the result of a shifting culture—it is the fruit of a silent church. We bear responsibility, by our timidity and by our failure to "preach the word in season and out of season." I would also suggest that the responsibility for blatant contradictions of scripture promoted by liberal, backslidden churches and denominations is also squarely on the shoulders of silent evangelicals who have allowed it to happen over the last century.

But there is hope. If we repent of our fear, reclaim our voice, and stand on God's Word, we can once again shape the future—not with arrogance, but with humility, conviction, and love. The world waits to see if the church in this generation will finally trade paranoia for courage, and pass on fruit that will remain (John 15:16).

Appendix

The following is a reprinting of two chapters from my book, *Things Your Church Would Tell You (...If They Could)*. It speaks to things pastors need to hear from many of their members. These are concepts gathered from our work in the US, Canada, and parts of Africa.

JUST SHOOT STRAIGHT WITH US—GIVE US THE TRUTH!

People: "Don't mince words, try to be WOKE, or worry about our feelings. Just 'preach the word'!
(2 Timothy 4:2)"

Several years ago, my wife and I planted a church made up of mostly teenagers. At one point, we had about 60 teens coming to events and about 20 adults. I wanted them to believe the gospel and have a relationship with Jesus. I was afraid that I would push too hard or too fast. I knew they faced temptations for sexual sin, drug use, alcohol abuse, and other sins daily. I knew that our culture was godless and anti-Christian, especially in Connecticut where our church did its ministry. I had them for a few hours a week, but the world had them 24/7.

So, needless to say, I was always looking for new and creative ways to reach and teach them. I remember having

Friday night, "Jesus Parties," where we would study God's Word, eat pizza (teenage manna from heaven), and pray together.

The first time we did this, I knew none of them had Bibles of their own. I had done research and found a VERY cool extreme sports/New Testament magazine that included the entire New Testament texts with articles about skydiving, bungee jumping, and other sports woven in. I also had a plain, leather-bound Bible in a modern translation I thought might work.

My plan was to show these to the teens and let them choose. Truthfully, I liked the sports magazine the best and assumed they would too. I was so proud of myself for finding it. I presented it with great enthusiasm and zeal, holding up a copy and pointing out the pictures of people jumping off bridges, etc. I did my best to sell it—I really pushed hard!

But, to no avail. After their listening patiently to my pitch, there was silence in heaven for the space of half an hour. Just kidding—it didn't take that long. When I was done, they sat staring at me for a moment and then one of them said, "PJ (my nickname, short for 'Pastor Joel'), could we maybe just have…a Bible? You know, just a regular Bible to read?"

I was so glad that I had brought a "Plan B" Bible to show them, and they quickly and unanimously chose it for use moving forward. I was surprised and a little embarrassed, but it was a great lesson that proved itself true over and over again in the years that followed.

What they were telling me, and what they repeatedly assured me was the case as we learned together, was this: THEY JUST WANTED THE TRUTH!

These kids, and the parents and adults that followed, didn't want me to equivocate, apologize, soften, or avoid anything God has for them in His Word. Even the new folks, who came through our doors laden with every kind of sinful lifestyle and problem imaginable, often just wanted to know what the Bible said. The more clearly and openly I shared it, the better!

Now, I realize that not everyone shares this desire. The key is that people truly pursuing God, and people saved and committed to Christ, DO want their pastor to be bold and share the truth. I tried to do that. This didn't mean that I was cruel or abusive in my approach either. I didn't beat them up or focus over and over on how angry God was/is or how sinful/evil they were so that everyone would leave feeling downtrodden and afraid. I preached a God of love and justice. A God who hates sin but loves sinners enough to die for them. I preached grace, hope, and salvation in the context of rejecting sin and sinful habits.

Yet, I learned to do this without avoiding things that might have been politically incorrect. I did this without apologizing for the Bible's tough stand on sex or other issues. And, I found that even when they struggled with some of this, my people appreciated the honest, open, no-holds-barred approach.

In our current ministry, my wife and I have the blessing of visiting leaders and churches across multiple denominations or independent evangelical circles. We serve in the U.S., Canada, Zambia, and Namibia, Africa, as well. While we witness many fine examples of pastors preaching the whole counsel of scripture, we also see the following:

- Leaders who avoid certain topics to escape being called "political." In other words, if a topic is in the news during an election cycle, they may refuse to discuss it. Abortion, for instance, is often in this category. It's as if politicians get "first dibs" on topics to cover and pastors have to stay clear. Nonsense! Who better to address this issue and ask people to vote in ways that align with scripture, protect the innocent unborn, etc.?
- Leaders who avoid certain topics to keep from "offending the new people." For example, pastors may refrain from addressing what scripture says about sex outside of marriage, homosexual lifestyles, transgender pressure from culture, or the whole LGBTQ+ agenda. It's as if they think these "new people" won't notice our conservative values until they're saved, and then we can sort-of slowly incorporate these things into our coaching

or discipleship approach. Some seem to feel people will "pick up" on these truths "by osmosis" and change their behavior after spending enough time in fellowship with other Christians. Again, nonsense! Not only do these strategies not work, it's really not what people want. My experience, via countless conversations with churchgoers, suggests that they just want the truth. They want to know what God says, and then they'll learn to deal with it. Sure, they'll need our help, but they want the truth.

- Leaders who avoid talking about tithing or giving to avoid being accused of selfishness or money-grabbing. This one is tough because none of us like being asked for money all the time. I remember attending worship at a nationally known church where they took three offerings. They had their usual offering, a separate offering for a missionary, and then because the pastor felt the first offering was insufficient, they held a third. I joked with a friend that they might grab us by the ankles, turn us upside down, and shake the loose change from our pockets before we left. But somewhere between that extreme and the silence many exercise about giving, lies the truth. A friend of mine was asked by a mentor, "Do you tithe?" "Why, yes," he replied. The mentor then said, "Does it bless you?" "Absolutely!" my friend responded, "In many ways!" The mentor smiled and then asked, "So then, why don't you want your church to experience those blessings?" His point was clear—if we believe that Luke 6:38 is true, why wouldn't we teach our people to be generous givers to the work of the gospel? If we know they'll be blessed, why feel guilty or ashamed of asking them to give? Just teach them the truth about this and trust God for the outcome!

I think sometimes we're like Tom Cruise and Jack Nicholson in the movie, *A Few Good Men*. Nicholson plays a hard-core Marine general and Cruise a Navy lawyer tasked with prosecuting a case of abuse during a hazing incident that lead to the death of a young soldier. While he's on the stand and under oath, Nicholson is angry at being interrogated. He feels his office/role had earned him the right not to have to be under such scrutiny. He asks Cruise's character what he wants, and with powerful passion, the lawyer states, "I want the Truth!" to which the general responds,

"YOU CAN'T HANDLE THE TRUTH!" Spoiler alert—if you haven't seen the movie, what follows is the breaking point in the case where Nicholson's character inadvertently confesses and Cruise wins the case.

As pastors, do we sometimes think our people "CAN'T HANDLE THE TRUTH"? I'm told by many of them that they can and that they want it. Sure, some will balk at things, and some might leave our fellowship because we're not WOKE enough for them. But my experience tells me that they would have left anyway—despite whatever efforts we may have made to avoid or soften certain doctrines. In fact, some are more upset that they WEREN'T TOLD UP FRONT about certain beliefs because they weren't open to these truths and never will be.

So, as Paul so aptly put it, we just need to "speak the truth in love" (Ephesians 4:15). Do it with grace and patience. Do it with love and concern. But Pastor—by all means—give them the truth!

PLEASE APPLY BIBLICAL PRINCIPLES AND WISDOM TO CURRENT EVENTS
AND TEACH US HOW TO DEFEND OUR FAITH.

People: "We need to know how to survive and thrive in our culture. We want to understand how to explain the relevance of the Bible to those around us and foster healthy change in our world. Help us impact culture with the gospel!"

At first glance, this chapter may seem to be a contradiction of what I wrote in chapter two. I assure you, I've crafted this carefully and even placed this chapter at the end of the book to be sure that it is NOT contradictory. The issue is one of focus. In chapter three, I'm encouraging a focus on the gospel. In this chapter, I'm encouraging that we focus on the whole counsel of scripture while making sure to show its cultural relevance, so that our people are well equipped for the Great Commission of Matthew 28:19–20. This is what I hear people asking for.

The days when pastors could pontificate about specialized nuggets of theology and use complex terminology to impress their churches are gone. As mentioned earlier, the days when we can avoid certain topics, in order to avoid being labeled as "too right wing," "too political," or "too conservative" are also well behind us. Finally, the option of only preaching "feel good" sermons that are emotive and solely focused on filling the front of the platform with an "altar call," no longer exists.

Change is here…and rightly so. Believers are rejecting these approaches…in droves.

Our world sees the church as largely irrelevant. I'm convinced that the only reason our socialist government in the U.S. has left the church alone in terms of much overt persecution is because our political and social leaders don't see us as much of a threat. Through our education system, the media/ entertainment industry, and good old-fashioned PR expertise, demonic leftist leaders have been able to steer our country and its culture with little resistance.

This demands we change!

Now, lest you think I'm suggesting that we abandon the scripture and use political talking points as sermon outlines, let me be clear. I believe that it is IMPOSSIBLE to preach the whole counsel of the Bible, while still focusing on the gospel, without automatically addressing things like:

- The sanctity of human life (thus, abortion, genocide, etc.).
- The primacy of Israel in God's plan (thus why we shouldn't give nuclear weapons/ technology to her enemies).
- The distinctives and value of men and women (thus rejecting gender neutrality or gender confusion).
- The unity and equality of the races (thus rejecting racism whether by the KKK or groups like Black Lives Matter, those promoting Critical Race Theory/CRM, etc.).
- The value of work and personal responsibility (thus combating large government/socialist/communist dogma).
- The Christian history of our nation and the British Commonwealth countries (thus destroying history revisionism).
- Tithing/giving generously (thus averting the tendency to give money to almost any cause, but not the church/ God's kingdom work).
- Marriage and family (thus destroying any possibility of supporting same sex marriages, sex outside marriage, and liberal parenting practices).
- The sufficiency and primacy of Christ and the gospel (thus renouncing ecumenicalism and the embracing of Islam, Buddhism, Hinduism, or other faiths as equals to ours.)
- God's focus on land/territory as a kingdom principle (thus destroying the "open border" concepts of the Left).
- Scripture's condemnation of intoxication (thus rejecting

the recent push to legalize and distribute dangerous drugs like marijuana or the lack of enforcement of laws regarding what can be easily transported across our border, i.e., fentanyl, etc.)
- And much, much more…

Far from being political topics, these are principles found from Genesis to Revelation. The only reason they don't get much airtime is our fear of attack by the Woke among us. But has this avoidance policy helped? Are our people more able to stand firm on principle and share how the Bible impacts everyday "real life"?

Absolutely not! In fact, just the opposite has occurred.

Apologetics aren't just for the apologists. I love men like J. P. Moreland, but the average citizen isn't going to read his books. They might, on the other hand, listen to you or someone in your church talk about WHY they believe what they believe.

Several years ago, I wrote a book called, *Walking to, and With…Jesus.* In it, I ask the reader a series of questions designed to lead him/her to a decision regarding Jesus and His work on the cross. I then lead the reader through a series of steps on how to grow in their faith. This book has been modified, or at least the second half of it has been edited, into a work called, Now What? where churches can put their own name on it and use it as a gift for people who have recently responded to the gospel with a faith commitment. (If you'd like to have a version of this made available under your church's name, etc., contact us at 860-938-2725.) I bring this up because isn't that what SHOULD happen with every believer—that they lead others through relevant questions which draw them to the foot of the cross?

Of course, it is.

The only way our flock will engage in this kind of activity though, is if they believe they are equipped to discuss the questions and challenging issues their friends and family may bring up. The topics I've listed here are no doubt on that list of questions/issues, as are others. But if pastors avoid those topics, how will our people be prepared/equipped for this task? Truth is, they won't be, and sadly, most aren't!

I'm a firm believer in exegesis. I preach expository sermons. But in addition to exegeting scripture, I also believe in exegeting culture. That is what many expository preachers do NOT do! I watch many current/popular movies. I listen to some popular music. I watch the news and listen to talk radio frequently. In fact, I'm even a guest host on a secular talk radio station.

Why?

I want to know what's happening so that I can teach people what the Bible has to say about these things. If I don't know what topics/issues are "hot," I can't do that. And, I'm just crazy enough to believe that my Bible is relevant no matter what demonic nonsense the Enemy might be pitching at the moment. I just need to open it and show people that. So…I do!

When I watch these movies or listen to pop music, I'm exegeting. I'm asking about the underlying message, motive, and methods. I want to be able to point out, for instance, that the reason every new drama on Netflix, Hulu, etc., has transgender, bisexual, and/or gay couples is that Hollywood has an agenda. They want us to believe that anywhere from 25–50% or more of humanity is involved in some kind of sexual deviance. Studies tell us it's more like 5%, but the push is for it to increase. To know and teach this, I have to be aware of it. That takes effort.

Unfortunately, my experience tells me that many preachers don't make this effort. Then they wonder why their people are so easily swayed by crazy, sinful, spiritually destructive temptations from the world around them. This has to stop! And, pastor, it's up to you and me to help stop this trend. I'm sure you agree that the Bible is relevant, perhaps even more relevant to what's happening in our world today, than ever before!

So…we just need to tell and show people that. And the good news is, most of them want to hear it!

Discussion Questions

NOTE: We believe there is safety in numbers. Thus, we encourage pastors and other leaders to discuss these concepts and their implementation with others. Here are some things to consider:

1. Do you agree with the basic premise of this book? Why or why not?
2. What has your experience been with fear regarding certain topics in scripture? How have you handled it?
3. Have you ever preached through the entire Bible exegetically? Why or why not?
4. If you've focused on certain passages or topics for sermons, what are some you have NOT covered and why?
5. What things have you done or seen done that allow the church to have a voice in modern culture or with political leadership?
6. Do you think Christians should vote? How have you encourage/discouraged this in the past?
7. Do you think Christians should run for political office? Why or why not?
8. While this book doesn't condone or promote a certain political party affiliation, do you think there is one party that tends to take positions more in line with biblical truth? If so, which one and why?
9. If you have members in your church who are more

liberal politically, what do they believe about abortion, sexuality, marriage, economics, and other topics covered in scripture? Regardless of party affiliation, do you think they need to better understand biblical teaching on these things? Why or why not?

10. If a pastor SHOULD avoid certain topics, what guidelines should he use? What are some examples of things that shouldn't be covered from the pulpit?

About the Author

Pastor Joel L. Rissinger and his wife Karen have been married for more than 41 years and have two adult children, a marvelous son-in-law, two gorgeous granddaughters, and three grandsons. No stranger to the change management process, Pastor Joel has worked as a consultant assisting Fortune 100 corporations with personnel and organizational change, marketing, and sales strategy. In the non-profit world, he has led three congregations through major restructuring including a three-way merger and two separate congregational mergers.

Currently, Joel is a Field Shepherd with Standing Stone Ministry where he and his wife provide coaching and encouragement to pastors, missionaries, ministry leaders and their families around the world. He is joined in that work by his wife Karen, a retired School Psychologist and Theology graduate. Joel is also the President of Joel Rissinger Ministries, LLC (JRM), an organization that provides training and support to churches through Joel's preaching, teaching, and writing gifts.

Prior to that Joel was the Executive Pastor at LifeWay Church and the Lead and Founding pastor of Mill Pond Church in Newington, Connecticut. Mill Pond started with fifteen people, mostly teens, in the Rissinger's living room in the summer of 2006 and grew to over 200 attendees.

Pastor Joel has a BA in Theology from Ambassador University, as well as MAs in both Religion and Religious Education from Liberty University. His writings include multiple published articles and the following books:

B.A.S.I.C Deliverance for Pastors
The Crucified Church
The Crucified Couple
The Crucified Life
Champion That Change
Communicate to Lead
The Death & Rebirth of Discipleship
Discipleship Without Discipline
Whole4Life
Now What?
Forgiveness Fallacies
Walking To...and With, Jesus
T.A.L.K. Your Way to Intimacy
My Three Mergers
Things Your Pastor Would Love to Say...(But Can't)
Things Your Church Would Tell You...(If they Could).

And, by Karen Rissinger:
Tapestry of Many Blessings

Endnotes

1. John Bevere, *The Awe of God*
2. Neil T. Anderson, *The Steps to Freedom in Christ*
3. Census of US Christians

Footnotes *Scripture and historical footnotes:*

1. Acts 5:27–29 ("We must obey God rather than men.")
2. See sermons by Rev. John Witherspoon, and works on the "Black Robe Regiment" in the American Revolution.
3. Matthew 5:14 ("A city set on a hill cannot be hidden.")
4. William Wilberforce led the British movement to abolish the slave trade, motivated by evangelical faith.
5. Dietrich Bonhoeffer, German pastor/theologian, was executed for resisting Hitler's regime on biblical grounds.
6. 2 Timothy 2:24–26 ("And the Lord's servant must not be quarrelsome but kind to everyone, able to teach, patiently enduring evil, correcting his opponents with gentleness…")
7.
8. See, e.g., Ligonier Ministries' State of Theology survey, showing confusion among U.S. evangelicals on basic doctrine (thestateoftheology.com/).
9. Reference for hospitality and boundary principle:
10. See: Leviticus 19 and Numbers 15 on treatment of foreigners; Ezra/Nehemiah on national boundaries; Proverbs 25:17 for common-sense boundaries; Matthew 25 on hospitality as a measure of faith.

Recommended Reading

Anderson, Neil T., *Victory Over the Darkness*,
Anderson, Neil T., *The Bondage Breaker*
Barnhill, Gena, *Simple Effective Prayer*
Barnhill, Press, *The Awakening*
Barnhill, Press, *The Battle*.
Rainer, Thom S., *Simple Church*, B&H Publishing Group
Rissinger, Joel L., *The Crucified Church*
Rissinger, Joel L., *The Forgiveness Fallacies*, Kindle Publishing.
Rissinger, Joel L., *Walking to, and With, Jesus*, Kindle Publishing.
Rissinger, Joel L., *The Crucified Life*, Kindle Publishing.
Barna, George. *Revolution*, Tyndale House Publishers.
Wilson, Jared C., *The Gospel-Driven Church*, Zondervan Publishing.

www.ingramcontent.com/pod-product-compliance
Lightning Source LLC
LaVergne TN
LVHW021410080426
835508LV00020B/2543